D1716788

Busy Machines

Rescue Vehicles

Written by Amy Johnson   **Illustrated by Steven Wood**

WINDMILL BOOKS™

Published in 2021 by Windmill Books,
an Imprint of Rosen Publishing
29 East 21st Street, New York, NY 10010

Copyright © 2021 by Miles Kelly Publishing

Find us on 📘 📷

Cataloging-in-Publication Data

Names: Johnson, Amy. | Wood, Steven.
Title: Rescue vehicles / Amy Johnson, illustrated by Steven Wood.
Description: New York : Windmill Books, 2021. | Series: Busy machines
Identifiers: ISBN 9781499485738 (pbk.) | ISBN 9781499485752 (library bound) | ISBN 9781499485745 (6 pack) | ISBN 9781499485769 (ebook)
Subjects: LCSH: Emergency vehicles--Juvenile literature. | Rescue work--Juvenile literature.
Classification: LCC TL235.8 J66 2021 | DDC 629.225--dc23

Manufactured in the United States of America

CPSIA Compliance Information: Batch BS20WM: For Further Information contact Rosen Publishing, New York, New York at 1-800-237-9932

To the rescue!

If there's an emergency, there are many kinds of vehicles that may come to help!

Engines ROAR...

Fire engine

Police patrol

On the go and on the lookout, these vehicles help the police do their jobs.

Dog unit car

Mobile command center

Motorcycle

Traffic car

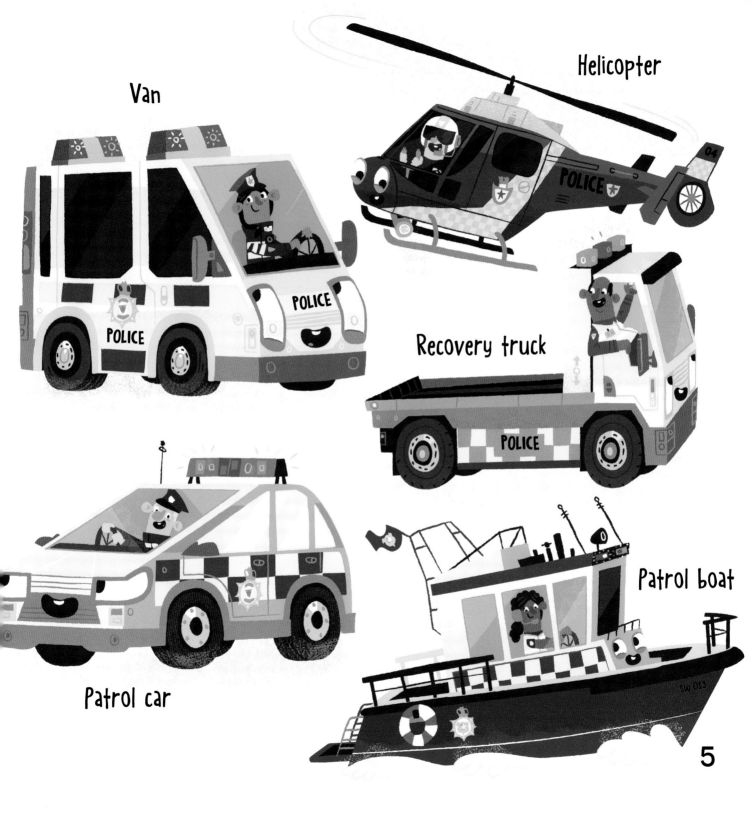

Van

Helicopter

POLICE

04

Recovery truck

POLICE

POLICE

POLICE

Patrol boat

SW 013

Patrol car

5

All about lifeboats

When people get into trouble on the water, a **lifeboat** will head out to help them.

The antenna picks up signals so the crew can talk to the lifeboat station and other boats.

Offshore lifeboats are used at sea. They're built to be speedy and to handle strong winds and waves.

Y-166

RNLI-11

Big lifeboats carry a smaller one for rescues in shallow water.

6

The lifeboat can quickly right itself if it capsizes! It has special water tanks that weigh down the bottom of the boat.

The boat sits low in the water so people can be easily reached.

The hull (body) of the boat is very strong.

SPLASH!

Ambulance in action

If someone is sick or injured, an **ambulance** must be able to reach them quickly.

Rapid response car

I carry machines and medicine to look after the patient until the ambulance arrives.

A **rapid response car** is used in some countries around the world to get places faster than an ambulance.

8

Speedy **paramedic motorcycles** can move quickly through traffic or along narrow roads. They are often first on the scene.

Paramedic motorcycle

Ambulance

Once the **ambulance** arrives, the paramedics get ready to move the patient inside.

9

Airport emergency

Planes carry tons of fuel, so a fire onboard is especially dangerous. Airport fire trucks can race to the rescue in minutes. They carry crew, equipment, and huge amounts of water and foam.

4

Water and foam are stored in here.

Hoses used by firefighters are in here.

Nozzles under the truck can put out fires on the ground.

The cabin can fit five crew members.

This sharp nozzle can punch through the wall of a plane. It is attached to an extra long arm.

WHOOSH!

Nozzles spray foam to smother the fire.

The heavy truck has six wheels.

11

Busy machines!

Pick your favorite rescue vehicle!

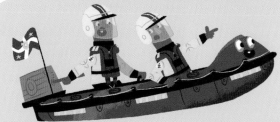

FIRE

DOG PATROL

POLICE

RNLI-11

13

Mountain rescue

Some climbers are lost in the mountains! A search and rescue crew gets to work to track them down.

Offroad trucks can take on steep, slippery ground. They carry stretchers and first aid kits.

A **minibus** carries rescuers and equipment.

All about ambulances

It's the job of an **ambulance** to get sick or injured people to the hospital as fast as possible.

Sirens and flashing lights warn other vehicles to move over.

The crew uses a radio to talk to the control center or hospital.

Ambulances have bright markings or symbols so they can be easily seen.

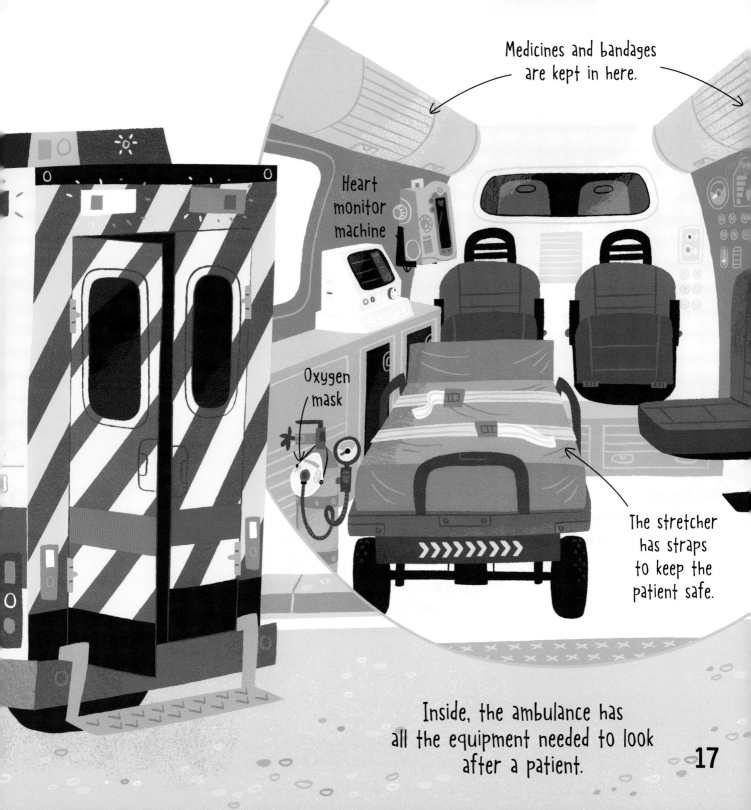

Medicines and bandages
are kept in here.

Heart
monitor
machine

Oxygen
mask

The stretcher
has straps
to keep the
patient safe.

Inside, the ambulance has
all the equipment needed to look
after a patient.

17

On the water

Climb aboard! On rivers, along the coast, and further out to sea, there are rescue vessels ready to help.

Offshore lifeboat

RNLI-11

Inshore lifeboat

B-756

Rescue hovercraft

Ship's life raft

Lifeguard rescue boat

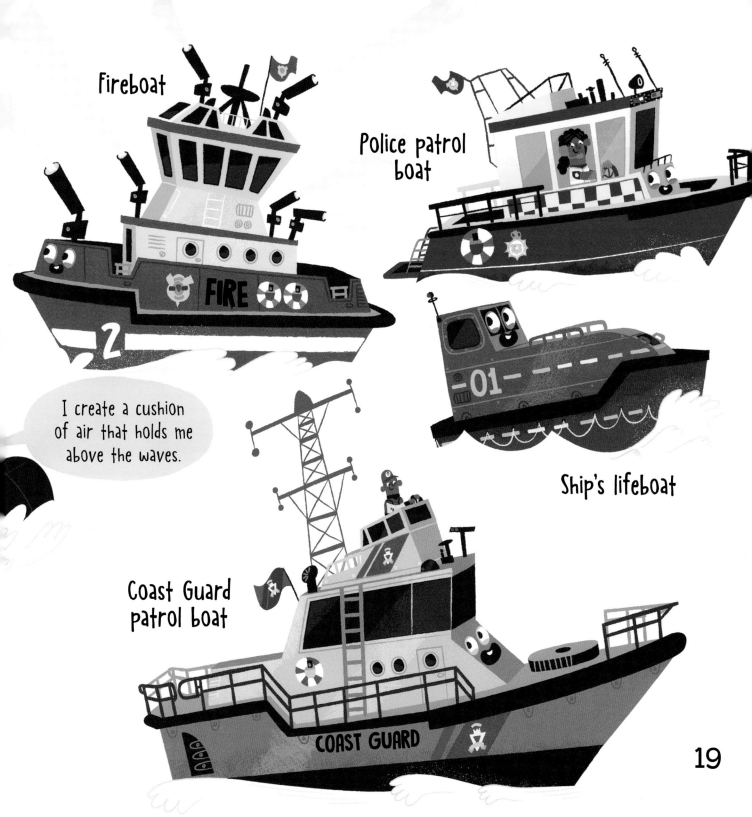

Fireboat

FIRE

Police patrol boat

I create a cushion of air that holds me above the waves.

Ship's lifeboat

-01-

Coast Guard patrol boat

COAST GUARD

19

Fighting fire

A fire is blazing, flames crackle and spark, but the fire engines are on the scene!

Firefighters work from the platform.

Ladder trucks have an extra long ladder that slides up to tackle flames in tall buildings.

Legs to keep the truck steady

Hose

20

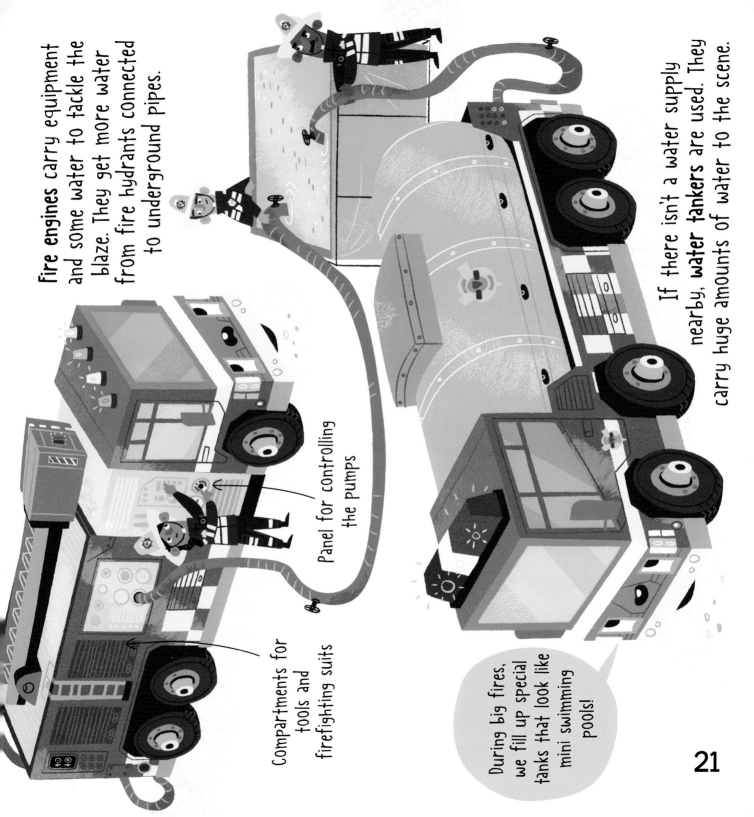

Fire engines carry equipment and some water to tackle the blaze. They get more water from fire hydrants connected to underground pipes.

If there isn't a water supply nearby, water tankers are used. They carry huge amounts of water to the scene.

Panel for controlling the pumps

Compartments for tools and firefighting suits

During big fires, we fill up special tanks that look like mini swimming pools!

21

Rescue flight

An **air ambulance** helicopter can reach sick or injured people and get them quickly to the hospital.

Firefighting planes drop water and special chemicals ahead of forest fires to stop them from spreading.

22

Search and rescue helicopters find people in trouble and make daring rescues.

Police helicopters help track down suspects, search for missing people, and keep an eye on big crowds.

It's easy for me to keep up with a speedy suspect!

Snow Searcher

Tough **all-terrain vehicles** are often used to rescue people stranded in heavy snow.

There is room inside for 17 people.

I'm great at snowy search and rescue, as I don't get stuck.

Two sections joined together move over drifts and slopes more easily.

Wide, tough tracks stop the vehicle from sinking.

24